This book belongs to

_____

Felix was a big black cat
With a coat, shiny and fine.
But he was a special cat
Because he **farted** all the time.

He never stopped all through the day
Which made his owners bitter.
Because everywhere that Felix went,
It smelled like **kitty** litter.

Felix was affectionate.
He loved to rub on legs,
But suddenly he'd fart so bad.
It smelled like rotten **eggs**.

Everyone agrees Felix farts a special one,
Especially when he's chasing mice.
It smells like stinky cheese.
But to them, it smells so **nice**.

The mice come running from their holes
Right into Felix's lap.
Attracted by the cheesy smell,
They fall into his farting **trap**.

Sometimes he climbs the curtains
Or sharpens his claws on the chair.
But suddenly Felix will fart,
And the smells **invade** the air.

Felix was taken to the vet
To have a **vaccination**.
So overpowering were his farts,
The vet went on vacation.

When Felix is out in the yard,
And birds fly down to eat,
He doesn't even chase them.
He just farts, and they **retreat**.

He shared the house with Max the dog
Who was not the least impressed.
Due to a dog's strong sense of smell,
Felix's farts made **poor** Max stressed.

One day, Max the dog chased Felix
Up and down the stairs.
Felix farted in his face,
So now Max hides under **chairs**.

Max soon gathered the courage.
He began to growl and bark.
But he soon yelped and ran away
When Felix farted in the **dark**.

Percy the Parrot lived there too.
He would stomp his feet.
When Felix farted near his cage,
It turned up Percy's **heat**.

"Felix my friend I must say,
Your farts are **stinky** - poo!
Go and find another home!
I need some space from you."

"Oh, you're such a silly bird!
Don't worry the smell will pass around.
My farts are more tolerable than
Your silly, screeching sound."

Percy the parrot escaped from his cage
And pecked at Felix's tail.
But that's a dangerous pursuit
Because his farts come without fail.

"Felix is a stinky cat...,"
Percy began to say.
The feline smiled and let one rip,
And the bird was blown away.

One night an evil burglar
Broke into Felix's house.
He knew the human family was out
And **tiptoed** like a mouse.

Max the dog just barked a bit,
And Percy said, "Who's there?"
"Percy wants a cracker!"
So the burglar wasn't **scared**.

He came to steal the jewelry
And any other valuables he could find.
The burglar searched and searched,
But there wasn't a lot of **time**.

He opened up the desk drawer
And found a money tin.
His eyes opened up widely.
There was a lot of **cash** within.

Suddenly, Felix was there in a flash.
He jumped up on the bench.
The burglar just dropped everything
When he smelled the **horrid** stench.

Felix was a hero.
He shared the fame with Max
And his friend, Percy the parrot,
Who had helped with the **attacks**.

Follow us on FB and IG @humorhealsus
To vote on new title names and freebies, visit
us at humorhealsus.com for more information.

@humorhealsus   @humorhealsus

www.ingramcontent.com/pod-product-compliance
Lightning Source LLC
Chambersburg PA
CBHW042025090426
42811CB00016B/1746